LETTERS FROM
THE BELLY OF THE WHALE
CONNECTING THROUGH COVID

Published by Hampshire Child and Adolescent Mental Health Service.
Profits raised from the sale of this book will support families using
Hampshire CAMHS through our official NHS charity "Heads On".

ISBN 978-1-8384970-3-3

Contents

Helen Dove

Dear Reader,

Thank you so much for buying this book. I hope you find plenty of inspiration, pleasure and humour in its pages.

It is a cliché, I know, to say that our young people are the future, but the experience of a global pandemic and a national lockdown has surely brought this into sharp focus. Hampshire Child and Adolescent Mental Health Service (CAMHS) is a specialist NHS service that works with young people up to the age of 18 with a significant mental illness. We all have mental health, all of us. Some days our mental health is good, and some days less so. A key building block for us all is learning to manage our own mental health, to nurture and care for it on a daily basis, just as we should our physical health and wellbeing. It is important to know what keeps us well, what to do if we sense ourselves sliding into unhelpful mood states, responses and behaviours, and, when necessary, knowing how and where to seek help. Finding time and opportunities to do things you enjoy, being creative, moving about and spending time with friends and family are vital to keeping ourselves emotionally and psychologically well.

An integral part of the spirit and ethos of our service development and delivery is listening to the voices of young people, whoever they are, wherever they are. At a time when households and communities across the country were closed down overnight, creating disconnection, fear, uncertainty, confusion and loneliness, it felt more important than ever to hear from our young people. It very quickly became clear that what we were experiencing was a once-in-a-lifetime event. This was global and affecting everybody, yet it felt inexplicable. The experience was not the same for everyone. Where you lived, your status, and situation had an impact. It seemed vital that this wide range of experiences was captured and shared to inform and connect.

Hampshire CAMHS reached out to young people via schools, youth organisations, and social media, inviting them to create a letter to share their personal experience of Covid and lockdown in whatever way they wished. This book is the culmination of a year-long project, during which time dozens and dozens of letters arrived from young people in Hampshire and beyond, all telling how it was for them, what they learned and what made their experience unique. Some adults were also invited to write open letters to young people affected by Covid. These voices seek to motivate and inspire a generation who have been uniquely touched by lockdown.

In relation to our own psychological and emotional health, promoting and providing time for creativity is so important and can have a massive positive impact. Creative writing as a means to connect, express and explore can bring great joy and positive wellbeing. This letter-writing project provided the opportunity to give voice to young people through their own creativity.

The experience has been humbling, exciting, and challenging, bringing both tears and laughter, and I am personally grateful to have had the privilege of reading every letter received. Sadly, it has not been possible to include every entry, but contained within this book are the letters, or parts of letters of 55 people. These letters mark the time frame between April 2020 and March 2021. The title for this book was inspired by the letter we received on page 25. Here the experience of lockdown is compared to the story of Jonah, who was swallowed into the belly of a whale. The organisers of this project felt it was such a clear visual way of understanding different people's journeys through the pandemic; perhaps you will agree when you come to read this letter. The selection and editing of the included letters has been a shared task, with Judy, Susmita, Charlotte and Abi, for which I am hugely grateful.

I hope you enjoy this book.

Helen

Helen Dove,
Lead for Innovations and Participation, Hampshire CAMHS

Dr Roopa Farooki

A Foreword, and Four Words

What a humbling honour it is to write the foreword for these brave, beautifully written accounts, bearing witness to our future selves, on what it was to live through the pandemic. These letters are an echo chamber of the difficult changes that were experienced, the sense of what was lost, and the moments of light, written with candour and courage.

Hampshire CAMHS (Child and Adolescent Mental Health Service) are the dedicated team who started this bold project, encouraging young people to reflect and write on what the time of Covid-19 has meant for them. We have accounts from children of all ages and communities, nine-year-olds who quite liked staying home and not rushing to school, eleven-year-olds who went through fasting at Ramadan and Eid celebrations without their wider families, teenagers who missed their friends and felt abandoned, young adults who had a keen insight into their deteriorating mental health. We have stories of honest helplessness, as these young people tried to manage their anxiety, their depression and eating disorders in these unprecedented circumstances, and their resilience, as they tell their stories, and open up a window into their lives.

I've had the privilege of being the junior doctor of young people dealing with their mental health during the pandemic; some have started their treatment journey with me in a GP office, I have looked after them as they came by ambulance into A&E, and in the hospital paediatric wards. I have spent time with them, at their bedside, taking their history, and listening to their stories.

So it is wonderful to see the letters of such astonishing patients fly out into the world, accompanied by the letters of their peers. They tell us about friendships, relationships, family, love, loss and loneliness, they tell us about their fears and ultimately, they promise us hope. These young people are writing their own truth, and sharing it with us.

I hope that you will read and learn as much as I did, from this kaleidoscope of communal experience.These are the personal stories that build bridges between us, and connect us in these strange times. That brave act of writing, that act of connection, is precious.

So these are the four words, with which I would like to close this foreword.

Listen to our stories.

Roopa

Dr Roopa Farooki is an NHS junior doctor, a Royal Literary Fund Fellow, and an Ambassador for Relate, the family counselling charity She is the award-winning writer of six literary novels for adults, published in over twenty countries, and has been listed for the Women's Prize for Fiction three times She won the Junior Doctor Leadership Prize in East Kent Hospitals for her work during the Covid-19 pandemic in 2020, and is the author of the *Double Detectives* Medical Mystery series for children, published by Oxford University Press Her novel *Everything is True*, a memoir of medicine, motherhood and mortality, is coming out with Bloomsbury in 2022

Elouise Paterson

Dear Future Me,

What happened in the year 2020? It all started when news of a new virus spread around. If you had a cough or a temperature you had to stay inside. Then the virus spread around and lockdown came into place and you could only leave for essential shopping trips. We all had to stay at home and online work became a thing. The days grew longer and longer and daily activities became boring. The cupboards started to look the same and mealtimes were a burden. Sleeping and dreaming became a new hobby for me. I dreamt about leaving the house, maybe just going to Tesco's but I knew it was not going to happen anytime soon. The infection figures started to go up, Boris was on my TV and the five o'clock briefing was something to look forward to. I woke up every day wondering if there would be a new restriction, would we be allowed out? Instead we got told that our stocks were running low. People all over started to panic buy and toilet paper was hard to find. Hand sanitizer became the new Gucci and the price kept going up. Small things around the house became exciting and I started to clean a lot. Soon restrictions started to ease and we could go for a family walk or ride a bike along the beach.

Now we are back at school and nothing seems the same, wearing masks in communal areas and sitting in numbered seats. If someone coughs in class, anxiety starts to appear. Will we be in the same situation next year?

Elouise Paterson
Age 14

Piper Stevens

Dear Future Me,

In 2020 we had lockdown because of Coronavirus, and had to isolate for weeks (in case you forgot) and mine was incredibly... boring. I missed being with my friends, some of my family, even being at school! All I really got up to was binge watching *My Hero Academia*, I mean, I did learn some Japanese from the show so that's quite cool, I also learnt a bit of voice pitching to match some of the characters (since I want and hope to be a voice actor). I did spend a lot of time with my mum, brother and sister and actually started to somewhat get closer to my siblings which is shocking. I did visit Dad from time to time but I didn't get to see him as much - unfortunately.

I did FaceTime Brooke, Grace and Ava a lot throughout lockdown and we played a ton of Roblox together and it was hilarious. We were all also preparing to go to school at the same time so we were all incredibly nervous.

I really hope you overdramatically tell your kids/grandchildren about this like Grandad would tell me stories. Make it sound like some crazy tale, even though it wasn't as insane as it seems.

Piper Stevens
Age 12

Dave Chawner

Dear Young People,

There's no gilding the lily, it's been rubbish - a global pandemic, GCSEs based on predictions, A levels uncertain and university admissions more ambiguous than ever before. That's even before you consider the mass redundancies, global recession and of course the tragic death toll. So you might well think 'what is there to be positive about?' Well, I'm here to tell you that there are things to be grateful for.

In March I lost my Dad. He wasn't old, 67. He got Covid and unfortunately didn't pull through. I was lucky enough to get to know Dad for 31 wonderful years. He was a great guy, small in stature but big in personality. I'm not the only person who's lost someone. But with that tragedy also comes an appreciation of the people who are left.

Yes, I know that sounds like some hippy dippy bull, but it's true. Think about it, a lot of the time you can only appreciate things too late, when they're no longer there. Whether that's health, wealth or happiness (or even just my PlayStation controller when my girlfriend has tidied up!). Losing Dad really made me feel appreciative of the people I had left in my life and motivated me to make the effort more.

But it's not only people. After lockdown I appreciate being able to go out and about whenever I want, rather than being restricted to once a day. When coffee shops opened people appreciated that first flat white in a while and when the restaurants threw open their doors it was great to see people enjoy their favourite food (without having to argue about who's doing the dishes!). It was exciting and heartening to see people appreciate the little things that we would otherwise take for granted.

And I'm not pretending things are all rosy and that I spend my days now sitting in a circle with all my friends and family singing 'kumbaya' and burning incense. There is a lot of uncertainty, I get that. And I'm not going to pretend that I know what you, personally, are going through.

Things might seem pretty intense right now. But it's not all doom and gloom and sometimes just knowing that things can and will get better is all you need. Keep going and don't give up.

Dave

Dave Chawner is a number 1 bestselling author, award-winning comedian, presenter and mental health campaigner. His book *Weight Expectations* was published in 2018

Scarlett Steele

Something else that has kept me busy is my diary/ journal. I don't write in it all the time, but every few weeks, to keep a record of what was going on at the time and how I was feeling. I wanted to do it so that I have something to look back on.

Scarlett Steele
Age 13

Sophie Broom

Dear NHS,

I am writing to you to tell you how my lockdown went. In my opinion, lockdown wasn't the best part of my life.

The first part I want to talk about is how amazing your NHS staff were. The amount of lives your crew saved was amazing. YOU made so many people and families happy. YOU saved their families' lives. YOU made their lives the best they could be. You should all be so proud of yourselves.

The next thing that I want to talk about is very heartbreaking for me because my dog got put down on April 23rd because she had a seizure and wasn't very well. We found out it was because she had a brain tumour and we had never known for the whole eight years we had her for. She was my best friend and wasn't even old. She helped me through everything. When I was sad, she would come to me and sit on my lap to give me a cuddle and to make me laugh. I'm just happy that she is in a better place now and that she is not in pain and is very happy. So that's why I would like to thank Vets4Pets as well because they always looked after her.

After that topic I would like to talk about how I was struggling with my anxiety. I was terrified to come back to school, I only missed it because it was easier than home school. Through lockdown I struggled a lot with my schoolwork as well so that didn't even help. School was really hard to the point I didn't do most of it because it was stressing me out, so when I got TWO postcards from school saying how good I was doing I was so happy because then that made me wanna do more of my work so I could get more postcards from my school. So that is why I want to thank all the teachers that helped me, especially Mr Groom.

The last topic I want to talk about is July 4th because on July 4th I got a new puppy called Daisie-Mae. She is a Maltese and is now five months old. She has been very loving and very, very fun to play with. She has lit up my world, it's like Sadie had been re-born after getting put down.

Thanks for reading this and I hope you get this,

Sophie Broom
Age 14

Anointed Afolayan

Dear Reader,

When lockdown suddenly started, I was a bit sceptical about what was happening. The news channels were going crazy about the new coronavirus, not to mention that it was spreading like wildfire around the world!

Once lockdown had started, you were only allowed to go out for food, exercise and medicine, which meant there wasn't going to be a whole lot to do. So, my family decided to get creative. Luckily, we have a trampoline in the back garden, so we didn't have to risk leaving the house to get exercise.

I enjoyed watching game shows on TV like *The Chase* and *Tipping Point*. Indoor bowling was another option. Me and my little sister would get a bunch of empty water bottles and fill them half-way. Then, we would arrange the bottles to look like a proper bowling set. Finally, using our living room passage as the bowling alley and a tennis ball we would take turns to bowl, tally up the scores at the end and see who won! Of course, you can guess who the winner would always have to be.

The way I see it, lockdown is a blessing AND a curse. On one hand, there is no school, although we do work at home. On the other hand, everything has been shut down and we have to stay in our homes. Despite the fact we can't go anywhere in particular, me, my sister and my dad would cycle to a few different places. Another thing I'm learning is piano. Sometimes my sister would play too, but not often.

The shutdown meant people were not allowed to go anywhere. A huge thank you to those who made it more bearable such as the bin man who took our bin and the delivery man who brought my mouse for my computer so I could play my games. Thank you to food shops that allow us to buy food so we don't go hungry and a gigantic thank you to the NHS for all the lives they have saved.

I hope Covid-19 goes away quickly. I also hope we will be allowed to stay at home after it goes away so that we don't have to wake up early and rush to school every day.

Anointed Afolayan
Age 10

Adam Ribi

Being in the same bedroom for six months is tiring, watching the same world go by is boring, wishing the same wishes is maddening.

Adam Ribi
Age 13

Lucinda Harris

Dear Reader,

This year has been a terrifying one, I believe the youth have been abandoned in our times of crises. We were told to stay home and to not see our friends, our families, our loved ones, we were told it was for theirs and our own safety. While we were at home we were not safe, families who needed help couldn't get it, my mum couldn't get her blood tests nor could she always get the right medication. We were the ones hiding from the world, no longer having our freedom or our independence. Their decision to shut down our schools for six months was a chaotic one as many students have fallen behind.

We had no choice, but their actions affected our lives, our futures and they believe this insanity they caused would not affect our mental health or our learning abilities. However it has, it has damaged so many of the youth and yet we did not receive the help we so desperately needed. When we needed the protection of the government we were shut out without a voice to be heard.

We were abandoned when we needed help. We were abandoned by those who were supposed to keep us safe. We were abandoned.

Lucinda Harris
Age 14

Melissa Taylor

Dear Diary,

Today is Tuesday 29th of September 2020, the year of the coronavirus worldwide pandemic.

Lockdown lasted for four months. From March until July. At first, I was excited to do my schoolwork at home in my pyjamas or comfy clothes. But after a month or so I wanted to go back to school and see my friends. During lockdown, George Floyd was killed by a white police officer who knelt on his neck for eight minutes and ignored his pleas for air. This has been all over the news for a few months. There have been lots of protests about 'Black Lives Matter'. This is not saying that all lives do not matter, it is just saying that until we are all treated fairly some lives matter more during one period of time.

Do you remember the year of 2020 and all of the things that happened?

Melissa Taylor
Age 12

Kadra Abdinasir

Dear Young People,

This year has been unlike any other with everything that's going on, from the Coronavirus pandemic, to the Black Lives Matter movement. And it's impacting us all here in the UK and around the world.

We've all had moments where we've felt worried, scared, sad, angry and frustrated in this period and some of us continue to have these feelings. This pandemic has really brought to light some of the ongoing challenges such as poverty, racism and discrimination that plague our society and perpetuate cycles of disadvantage.

Yet despite everything, all of this, it has really warmed my heart to see young people from across the nation coming together to use their voice to speak out about the issues they care about. From challenging racial inequality to fighting for fair exam results, you are all making your voices heard loud and clear. You have shown us the power of digital and social media during this time to tell your stories, make us laugh and shine a spotlight on important issues.

You support and show solidarity to one another, regardless of race, gender, sexuality, disability, and status in society. You stand up in the face of injustice, inequality, and adversity because you want brighter futures and want lasting change for the next generation. You're willing to listen and learn (much more than us adults!) and are open to doing things differently (hello digital learning). This has truly inspired me.

Things may seem difficult and uncertain at the moment but you remain hopeful and see the light at the end of the tunnel. Your ongoing determination and resilience is what we need to help us all get through this period and find solutions to some of the key issues of our time.

I want to let you know that you're not a 'Covid generation' or a 'lost and forgotten generation' - you're much more than that. You are part of the generation that will break barriers and help us create a more fair and equal society where we can all be our true authentic

selves and prosper.

Kadra

Kadra Abdinasir is Head of the Children and Young People's programme and strategic lead for the Mental Health Coalition

Chloe Lockyer

Dear Reader,

My name is Chloe, aged 17. My time during the lockdown has been different to others', I think - my anxiety has calmed down because I am not out in society trying to be someone I am not. Instead, I am sat at home, blasting out my music that I love and lounging around in my pyjamas with cups of tea trailing one after the other. I have depression and high anxiety, so for me, this lockdown has brought a miracle to some aspects of my mental health because I feel calmer, I can enjoy the things I love while other people usually judge me. I really enjoy being the real me.

However, even though it sounds like I am having a good time 24 /7, it really is not the case. I still freak out because this feels continuous and is going to be forever. I still have panic attacks and I am quite lonely even though I live with my family. But eventually this will end because we need to return to normal again. With the support from my family, they compose me and make me feel okay again, which I cherish because they are supporting me when they have never been through this before, but it shows that we are all in this together!

A lot of the time I use my self–soothe box as my therapist told me to do and it keeps me entertained. I keep soft things in there and a candle so that when I smell or feel things, I feel calm again. 😊 I have been doing painting, reading and decorating and definitely learning more about home economics because I understand I need to keep myself busy and to distract myself. It's been really fun!

If my future self is reading this eventually, I do not know when, but I want to tell myself that I did so well at composing myself during a hard time, and that I kept going in order to survive a pandemic! This has been such a difficult period that I am surprised I made it, but it shows I can now do anything. So, I hope future me reads this and feels good about herself and knows that she has the power to do anything. 😊

Chloe Lockyer
Age 17

Ela Jolliffe

My Lockdown

Looking at the birds in my garden,
Oven filled with my cooking,
Cookies that I make taste mouth-watering,
Kitchen with me and my dad baking.
Dictionary reading,
Outside on my swing,
Working hard on school work with my mum, but
Not much fun without my friends...

Ela Jolliffe
Age 9

Naomi Gilchrist

Dear Reader,

Right now it might feel like you're in a really dark place and that you've fallen down a big hole which makes you feel hopeless, lost and trapped and you're not sure how you will ever be able to get out of this hole.

Whatever you set your mind to achieve you will get there, you've just got to trust and put one foot in front of the other and if you need to stop that's okay and if you want to run or dance, go for it.

Naomi
Age 27

Naomi Gilchrist is an ambassador working with Beat a National eating disorder charity

Lewis

Dear Reader,

When this all started in March, I was full of questions: how would I do my work? When would I see my friends again? Would my family be OK? Now, three months on since lockdown began, I have been spending lots more time with my family - it's been fun most of the time but I have argued with my sister a bit. Every week we have a treat dinner as a family and once a week we have a FaceTime chat with Nan and Grandma and Grandad. It took them a while to work out how to use it, but they are experts now! I like chatting to them but it's not the same as being able to give them a hug :-(

Lewis
Age 10

Selina Ullah

Dear Young People,

As we come to the end of Ramadan and the government talks of easing the lockdown, I began to think more about Prophet Yunus (Jonah) in the belly of the whale.

Like Prophet Yunus, we too have been in the belly of the whale: our lockdown Ramadan. We have gone through various emotional states. We have experienced initial confusion about our situation, the change in our environment, the enforced restrictions limiting our existence and everything we took for granted. Fear followed. Many of us were frozen by the fear of the sheer magnitude of what we faced as humankind. While many talked of how this was a wonderful opportunity to improve ourselves, discover new skills and talents and connect with God, we could not forget those numbed by pain, fear, mental illness and abuse and who remained locked in a state of fear – made worse by this new lockdown life.

As the weeks passed, the fear has turned to reflection. Prophet Yunus reflected on his situation - he overcame his frozen state of fear and he asked for forgiveness, repented, and accepted that his purpose was to spread God's message. And like Prophet Yunus, we too have the opportunity to reflect, repent and amend our ways. Ultimately it is a realisation that we have to change, and to do this we have to think and act differently. We have been too busy juggling all the work/life demands, actual and perceived. Often, we have not juggled very well, inevitably neglecting some aspects, be that ourselves, family, neighbours, or God.

So, while in the belly we have practically done our bit: we maintained social distancing, even keeping our distance from those we want to hold closest; we looked out for others, checking in on our friends, neighbours and family members and we volunteered, picking up shopping, organising meals and picking up prescriptions. We expressed our gratitude for all that we have by doing for others. We behaved differently because we had time to reflect. We were able to cut out the background noise so that we could hear our inner voice.

Lockdown Ramadan gave us time to pray with our immediate families in a deeper way and seek spiritual solitude as required. The veils were lifted from our eyes so that we could see that we don't need as much as the adverts tell us we need. Our lives haven't drastically taken a dive because we don't have the latest gadget, or beauty treatment, and we learned there are more meaningful ways to spend our money in the service of others.

As we leave the belly of the whale and bid farewell to the blessed month of Ramadan let us leave with a realisation that Ramadan in lockdown has been a blessing for many of us. That while being in the belly of the whale, we have achieved a sense of our purpose, gratitude for the enormous privileges we have, a strong sense of responsibilities for others and to others. If there is one thing the belly of the whale has taught us, it is that as humans we are connected much more intrinsically than we ever thought. May we all leave the belly of the whale intent on taking positive action and change for the better.

Selina

Selina Ullah speaks up against injustice and inequality and wants to make a difference. She is a proud Northerner of Bangladeshi descent, a mother and a grandmother who loves eighties new wave music, old Hollywood films and travelling

Rahmat Ismail

Dear Future Me,

I write in the hope that you will find this letter and read it.

Do you remember the ninth month of the Islamic calendar and celebrating Eid at the end of it during the stay-at-home lockdown? You probably do since life in 2020-2021 (and probably further, I don't know) was a BIG DEAL. Usually I/you would go to the masjid to pray Eid Salah, visit people as it is a usual custom on this occasion and go out and about meeting people, but this time is way different.

Days before the 29-30 day, we went to the shops to buy sweets and treats for other families to leave at their doorsteps as we were not allowed to go into other people's houses at the time. As well, my/your former teacher, Sister R came round the night before and dropped me and Yusif some sweets and goody bags for us to have. She stayed a two-metre distance away from our door and we could not embrace her to thank her due to Coronavirus social distancing measures at the time.

On the day the end of the month of Ramadan was announced, we prayed Eid Salah at home as a family unit. This was the first time in my life we followed a sheikh on a live YouTube Family Event channel, who advised us what we could do for Eid in lockdown. Mum cooked rice with meat which was really good. Mum also gave us ten pounds each as a present. A good friend of Mum's also got delivered to us three boxes of Islamic games as a present. We made several Eid greetings phone calls to my many grandparents, aunts, uncles, cousins, family friends, teachers, etc. As the day progressed, together me, Mum and my brother watched TV, had fun games, ate delicious food and sweets, though we couldn't go to the park as we usually would for some fun due to regulations.

In a flashback, fasting in the month of Ramadan was sort of the same too. Past you, past Yusif and past Mum did our best to offer voluntary prayers and listened to Bashir Ahmed Masjid's weekly Friday khutbah live on Facebook. Usually we would drive to the masjid to break our fast there with other people at the time of salat-al-Maghrib, and me/

you and past/present Yusif late in the evening would return to pray the 8-20 rakaat tarawih prayer. But this time we did it all at home instead. We fasted from sunrise to sunset whilst praying and reading the Qur'an. Do you know in 2019, I'd fast at school during the school hours, skip lunch and come home to break my fast. I was sort of lucky that lockdown was initiated because that way I could fast at home.

Hope things are good for you in the future/present!

Rahmat Ismail
Age 11

Tayyaba Rauf

Dear Reader,

How can I even begin to tell you what a strange and surreal experience Ramadan and Eid were this year, how much we missed the hustle and bustle of family, the common bond of forming the resolve to fast from dawn to dusk, the waking up in the middle of night to prepare 'sehri' (morning meal) for everyone, keeping each other going during the hunger and thirst all day, of again congregating in the evening to prepare the 'iftari' (food to break the fast) and then of course breaking the fast together at sunset. All our lives we have associated Ramadan with family and sharing the experience together. This year however, it felt rather alien. We had to celebrate Eid by ourselves. What celebration? How can one celebrate anything alone? There is no joy in that! It was heartbreaking not to have the elders in the family start the food preparations the minute the Eid moon was sighted at the end of the thirtieth fast.

Going to the mosque alone on the morning of Eid to offer prayers was very bizarre as one associates that with last minute commotion of large families trying to congregate and leave the house together, someone always running late, someone who can't find their prayer mat, always amidst laughter despite the chaos. The laughter, the tête-à-tête, the camaraderie, the happy pandemonium, the never-ending partaking of food and tea, this is what Eid is all about, and this is precisely what we missed desperately during the lockdown!

God willing, next year will bring better tides and we will all be able to celebrate the joys of Ramadan and Eid together. Take good care 'til then.

Yours,

Tayyaba

Tayyaba Rauf is a cover teacher and matron at Kings' School Winchester and mum of three teenage boys

Ethan Edmonds

Dear Future Me,

I can't wait to start playing football again with my team. Training is starting soon but we can't touch anyone so it's going to be very hard. We can't play matches yet either. My favourite team Tottenham Hotspur are playing a match tonight for the first time in three months. I'm going to watch it on TV! It will be weird though as no supporters are allowed to go, so there will be no shouting or cheering!

See you later!

Ethan Edmonds
Age 9

Joseph

Covid-19 was a horrible, HORRIBLE disease.
Joseph
Age 7

Simon Barber

Dear Students,

Hey team. What a year this has been! I hope we'll see each other soon - it seems like such a long time since I've welcomed you into my room - a little too cheery so early in the morning - and asked if I'm keeping you up when you come in yawning. I don't miss arguing over untucked shirts or trying to hassle you to do your work but I do miss your eye-rolls and your groans and your "don't!" at my awful 'dad' jokes and my long anecdotes. And there's two ways to feel about missing some things - don't get me wrong, there's more that I miss than going to work and seeing you kids - but whatever it is, those things that you miss, you can be bitter and grumpy when they're no longer with you, or you can see with perspective and treat them with gratitude. For me, the latter's the much better attitude.

And sure, yes, it's hard, you've not done this before – but maybe that's something to be grateful for. The challenge we're facing now every day is an opportunity when you look at it the right way. We must not focus on what we have lost, or worry about what it might have cost, but focus instead on what we have learned, be grateful for whatever we've earned. So what did you gain? How have you grown? Independence, resilience, patience, endurance, perseverance, perspective, creativity, nuance – the list goes on and I could list them again and they're different for everyone, no-one's the same. You are all now already equipped with the strengths I took years to learn and you've done it in months – you're not behind on learning, you've got a head-start! Seeing it that way is the real art.

So do not lose hope or be beat into submission; rise to the challenge, step up to the mission. Use this time wisely, reflect on yourself, protect your emotional and physical health. Work hard at your work, rest hard at your rest, enjoy the small moments and search for what's best, talk to your parents, talk to me too, look out for each other, we'll look out for you. Stay safe out there, don't go out of reach,

I'll see you all soon,

Be good,

Mr Teach

Simon Barber is English & Media Team Leader at Perins School, Hampshire

Jessica Mae Dowell-Lucas

To the NHS,

I am writing to you about my experiences during the lockdown.

I remember watching movies and Friday night camping in the living room. At one point during the lockdown I thought I would never see my friends again, or any of my teachers. But when my mum and dad told me that I could go to school for three weeks before I started secondary, I was overjoyed because I knew that on Monday, I would be going back to school.

I learnt how to grow my own vegetables such as salad, carrots and cucumber. I will tell my grandchildren in years to come about how fun it was to do home schooling with my mum and how important it is to spend time with family.

I would love to thank all my family (my mum, dad and my sister Sofia) and friends who have cheered me up throughout the lockdown. Also I would like to thank all my school teachers, because over lockdown they had been sending out work for people to do at home.

It was quite hard for me during the lockdown because my mum has been shielding and my dad is a key worker (he works down at Southampton docks), so I have had to take extra precautions. Also I found it quite hard not being able to see other family members because I love seeing my family.

My sister and I couldn't do swimming lessons because the leisure centre was shut. When we started going out to places we had to social distance, two metres apart, as well as making sure to put hand sanitiser on our hands.

I loved doing Clap for Carers, because we got to show how grateful we were to you and everyone else, who were looking after people during lockdown.

My mum and dad would watch 5pm news briefings every night and I would say to them, "not this again" but they would say "it is really important sweetie".

I remember when in lockdown we got online food shopping deliveries and once we received them, my mum would wipe all of it down to be safe (we even still do it now).

We also painted pictures of rainbows to put on our windows, to bring some happiness to people's lives in this hard time.

I remember spending VE Day in lockdown and we put flags up on the windows and spent the whole afternoon before VE Day outside colouring in pictures of the army.

I got a bit worried when I started back at school, because I had all these questions in my head, like "is it going to be safe?" and things like that, but when I started back there I found that there are ways that you can stay safe:

- Wearing a mask while walking around school
- Putting hand sanitiser on before and after all my classes
- Trying to stay two metres (six feet) away from other people when you can
- Singing songs to make sure I am washing my hands properly.

Yours sincerely,

Jessica Mae Dowell-Lucas
Age 12

Abigail Osborne

My Lockdown

I lost track of time and days
I miss my friends and family
I found time to sing not just one song but five songs.
Mum and I spend our afternoons with Gareth Malone
Singing 'You Are My Sunshine'
Thinking of the wonderful time I had with my Granny and Nanny.
'This Is Just Another Storm'
Yes it is because it will pass soon for me to give my hugs to my Nanny and Granny
Love you both
Thank you Gareth Malone for teaching me these songs.
Kept me busy and out of Mum's hair.

Abigail Osborne
Age 9

Brooke Relph

I thought Covid-19 would be great because it would take me away from my school, but instead, it took me away from the world.

Brooke Relph
Age 10

Meriel Anderson

Dear Reader,

I was in my first year of university near Brighton when Covid-19 was first declared a pandemic. Along with the majority of my peers, I didn't think it would affect me too much. However, when my mum insisted on packing up my student room and the campus began to empty, I figured it had to be more serious. Looking back, I had probably already contracted the virus, I just didn't know it at the time. I wasn't ill, but I lost my sense of taste and smell for a few weeks. Later, we learned that this is a frequent symptom.

I spent the first lockdown at home with my mum and my older brother. I occupied myself by going for long walks and watching endless TV shows – it was difficult to focus on my coursework. When restrictions eased, I was ecstatic to be able to move into my first student house in Brighton, and for a couple of weeks in the autumn things felt almost normal. Then came lockdowns two and three, by which time learning had moved completely online.

Brighton is usually so loud and vibrant, its narrow lanes crammed with shoppers, so to see it empty all of a sudden was such a shock to me. A few people continued to walk or run along the beachfront, but the buses ran without passengers, and for a long time the city was eerily quiet. All day I sat at my desk in my room, reading or studying – we called it 'Zooni'. At night, however, I loved walking along the desolate streets when all the seagulls had gone to bed. Being locked down in a big city is a very strange experience, but at times I found it profoundly peaceful. The air seemed cleaner, although the rubbish from disposable cups soon piled up, as cafes could only serve take-away drinks.

Now that the city has re-opened, the buses are filling up again and the traffic jams and the fumes are building. I long for the energy and excitement to return to Brighton, but those night-time walks were special. I think I'll always enjoy walking in the early hours, when the city falls quiet.

Meriel Anderson,
Age 20

Diana Burch

Dear Reader,

The day we locked down, I felt that everything was disappearing from me. I wouldn't be able to see the people I wanted to, do the things I enjoy – and I was scared of what the Coronavirus might do to us all. I had to cross out all of the things I had in my diary as one by one, all events were cancelled.

My work is important to me and you would think being an artist it would be ideal to be unable to leave the house! But at least half of my work involves working alongside others - often young people - helping them to find their creativity and give them a voice by finding the right ways for them to express themselves.

That time felt full of frustration and fear, and in its way, those feelings drove away my creativity ... and that made me feel even worse. So I started to walk (that's the thing that I do to solve things, it gives me thinking space). You remember we had a beautiful spring? We had time to notice things like birdsong and wildlife and to stop and stare at nature. Nature just carried on doing its thing, like nothing was any different. I found that inspiring and started to draw again – nothing grand, just about the things that I was noticing. And I started to feel better.

I know that doing creative things can make people feel good, it's part of my job! But it took me a while to apply it to myself. Once I did that, I realised I could share that good feeling with others in lockdown, so like many people I went online to start a creative community project. Through that I was back in touch with people again, and meeting new ones. Not in person, but in the New Normal.

Technology allowed a huge explosion of ordinary people taking part and sharing their arts projects. That could be anything from painting and drawing, to learning a new craft, making music, dance or humorous videos. They all take that crucial thing we all have – ideas. Ideas make us human, and arts are the way we can share them with other people.

The key is to make that brave start. Work with the things that interest you. Make that little sketch, write those few words, record your tune hummed into your phone. Once you have something to work with, you don't have a scary, blank page any more. And then the ideas start to come. It doesn't have to be about a career, but it will be about you – and you and your ideas are important. Who knows where they might lead?

Stay safe and look after yourself,

With my best wishes,

Diana

Diana Burch is a visual artist with a socially engaged practice

Sophia Grove

Dear People of the Future,

I would imagine I do not need to tell you what has happened at this time in history but I will give you a perspective of a regular person.

Let's start with my daily routine: I get up, brush my teeth, have a shower after my run and put on my clothing. My mother is home schooling myself and my brother; the location is my dining room!

One day a week at 8pm, we clap the NHS - National Health Service. I blow a whistle too, as I know what they are all doing is at their own personal risk. We sometimes interact with the neighbours over the fence, asking if they are all ok and need anything. Much else rarely happens, the odd drive to local shops, the odd text or call to my friends who also seem a bit lost.

On my days when I am not doing schoolwork, I enjoy writing, sewing, art and especially making up fabric masks. My mum asks me to sit in the sun for a while to get some vit D as we need it to stay healthy.

So far this has been a difficult time for me but I try to keep as happy as possible. I want to believe that whoever reads this letter in the future will be able to say yes, it was a nightmare that came true but we got through it.

Sophia Grove
Age 14

Deborah Neubauer

Dear Young People,

Creativity has been a lifeline during lockdown, using it as a way to express ourselves and connect to the outside world. People across the globe have been united in joining each other through online drawing, dance, music, writing classes and so much more. Art supplies have also been sent to thousands of people across the UK, providing the opportunity to be creative and explore new ways of self-expression. Arts and culture have also reconnected communities and allowed people's voices to be heard about important issues, most noticeably the #BlackLivesMatter movement, during lockdown.

Lockdown has proven that, even in our darkest times, arts and culture can provide many positive benefits that support our mental health and wellbeing and provide a platform for everyone to share their voices in an accessible and creative way. As we continue in these unprecedented times, we can be sure that we can rely on arts and cultural activity to enable us to continue learning new skills, express ourselves, share in our achievements, and provide an outlet for self-exploration; in turn improving our mental health and wellbeing.

With best wishes,

Deborah

Deborah Neubauer is Head of Community at Hampshire Cultural Trust

Samuel Munday

Dear Reader,

Author Jhumpa Lahiri once said that books 'let you travel without moving your feet', and rarely has an idea been more important than during a year in which so many of us have been stuck at home.

One of the things that's always kept me grounded in times of difficulty is the power of stories. The idea that, for one quiet moment, however brief and however I feel, I can transport myself to a faraway place and make new life-long friends, by simply opening a book.

Fiction gives us so much. It can open our eyes to new possibilities, allow us to explore ourselves through others, entertain us, thrill us, make us laugh, cry and love, and all the while allow us space to breathe, away from the chaos of everyday life. 'A book is a little empathy machine', as author Neil Gaiman puts it, full of endless knowledge and wonder, and the fact there is somewhere we can access all this for free is sublime.

During lockdown my colleagues and I at the library where I work have been diligently picking books for customers, because we understand the important role books and libraries play in our community's mental health. People fill out a form online and tell us what kind of genres and authors they like to read. We then hand-pick titles using our expertise and bundle them into surprise packages for them to collect. A sort of blind date with a book! So many people are turning to the comfort of stories to get them through these uncertain times.

But sometimes more serious books are needed too. Lockdown closures have presented a unique challenge when it comes to topics such as mental health. When we don't feel ourselves, it can be daunting or even embarrassing to ask for books that might help, and as our own safety often means we are unable to browse at the moment, it makes it that extra bit harder. That's why, at the library where I work, we make non-fiction titles as accessible as possible for all ages and backgrounds. By showcasing a diverse range of inclusive material, promoting national health campaigns such as Children's Mental Health Week and sign-posting important organisations such as

Young Minds, who are there to help in a crisis, I hope that everyone will be able to find what they are looking for when they need it most.

Let's take a moment to appreciate libraries and all that they do. Whether it is providing contact to our Home Library Service users, or hosting charities who support young people with learning difficulties, we strive to make our libraries an inclusive and welcoming place for everyone. For many the library is a safe place to chill, relax and find the support they need, and that means closures have been difficult, but rest assured we are still here and eager to welcome you back when the time comes.

For now, let's stay safe, support those around us and indulge a little in the power of storytelling. You never know what fantastical places you might visit from the comfort of your own home!

Best wishes

Samuel

S.J.Munday currently works as a Library Team Assistant at Winchester Discovery Centre, and is also a children's writer, poet and freelancer with a love for all things fantastical

Hannah Glyde

Dear NHS,

Quarantine caused my anxiety to get worse by raising my panic attacks from getting them once every few weeks to at least twice a day. I missed my grandparents and friends a lot but I did FaceTime and texted them a lot.

However, I did enjoy my extra free time which I spent reading around twenty books over the lockdown and watching my favourite movies and programmes, e.g Marvel, *Hunger Games* and *Brooklyn 99*. I also spent a lot of time choreographing dances and writing scripts I would perform to my pets.

When I first saw my grandparents again, I felt awkward and out of place as I had got so used to talking on the phone, I had forgotten how and what to talk about. After more visits I got more used to the two-metre rule and we compromised. For example, for my mum's birthday we had a BBQ outside with the family and they brought their own chairs which they sat on.

My quarantine was stressful, but we compromised which I am thankful for.

Hannah Glyde
Age 14

Edith Lumley

Dear Reader,

Lockdown is hard.

I miss everyone. My friends, my teachers and the school itself.
And I miss seeing my family. My grandma and grandad.

I want to get out of the house. I want to run and play at a park.

I know I can't. I know people are getting sick so we have to stay safe.
Stay home.

I'm scared for a second wave. I don't want more people to die.
It's sad when people die. It makes your heart hurt.

I did like my sister's birthday. We saw Grandma and Grandad.
They came to the house and waved at us. They blew kisses and left
presents on the doorstep.

I find video calls hard. It makes me miss people more after them.
I miss hugs.

I want to go to school again but I don't want to be socially distant.
I don't want plastic between us. I don't want to be alone and not
near people.

I like being able to stay up late and having no alarms.

I love spending time with my mummy. I can hug her all the time.
That makes me happy. But I don't have many happy things.
Some days I'm just down and not happy.

That is my letter. That is how I feel about Covid 19 stuff.

Edith Lumley
Age 8

Harry Le Rougetel

To Daddy,

Lockdown has been a fun time because I got to do the van with you. And I feel happy and sad that you have to go back to work. I liked doing the van with you because I like doing mechanical stuff and spending time with you.

I have enjoyed watching *The Mandalorian* with you because I get some free time with you.

Things I like doing with you:

- Bike rides
- Doing my mini rocker
- Ripping out Nanny's kitchen
- Doing Lego with you
- Map

Though I have missed the family, I have liked spending time with you.

Love,

Harry Le Rougetel xx
Age 9

Harvey Cook

To All,

This is a letter from me when I was experiencing lockdown. It has been a different experience for sure, and is not something I am completely used to.

I worry about how other people are getting along during this time, certainly close friends and family. You can understand, my closest relatives live a two-hour drive away, and I have not seen them since late February. I am also worried about the government letting up lockdown restrictions. (I don't know if I am allowed to talk about this.) I feel like if the government releases lockdown restrictions, people are just going to carry on as normal. They have no way of knowing if they have the virus or not (because of the incubation period) and I feel like the virus will start to spread faster again. I already know people who are just meeting up like nothing matters, and it scares me, because I think things will start to get worse than they already are.

I am not feeling certain on what is to come, but given the state of 2020 so far, all we can do is follow the rules and hope Corona kind of just dies out.

I hope this makes sense, but yeah thanks for reading,

Harvey Cook
Age 15

Dr Lia Jones

Dear Young People,

It's safe to say that 2020 has not been what anyone had been expecting. This letter is written to anyone who has found, or is finding parts of this year difficult. This is to anyone who has experienced disappointment or has had to adapt to new or unfamiliar things. You are doing brilliantly, and you are not alone! It is the community and togetherness that has kept us going all this time and will continue to keep us going. I am going to share my story of the past few months and then hopefully you will share yours with me, and we will slowly but surely put the pieces back together and realise we have plenty to be thankful for still!

This year began with me having my final exams for medical school – lots of studying and not much going outside, even before lockdown. This was the last set of university exams between being a student and being a doctor and required a lot of studying. After exams we had plans for an amazing summer, involving holidays, a wonderful graduation, and relaxing with friends. I had never been more excited for anything. I had spent many years thinking about how amazing it would be to finally graduate. Unfortunately, COVID arrived during our exam season, so for a while I did not know if I would become a doctor at all. You may have seen on the news that many medical students graduated early so that they could work on the wards during the summer – I was one of them. I felt nervous and a bit unprepared, but I wanted to get involved. It ended up being a great learning opportunity and I am so glad to have been able to use my time to help out. I am now a junior doctor on the hospital ward and it is a steep learning curve but I am having a brilliant time.

For those of you back in school now – how does it feel? I'm sure lots of things will be different – your teachers may be wearing masks, you won't be able to play with your friends in the same way, and you may not be able to move around the school like you used to. What hasn't changed though, is how much your friends will have missed you. How loved and important you are. How your teacher wants what is best for you, and how your learning and education is the most important thing! For those of you who may have lost their university place or had to take a different route, I am sorry this happened. You can take whatever route you need to, you will still get there with the right work, and there are plenty of people to support you.

It is valid if you are feeling upset and confused, we are still feeling the effects of COVID and it will take a while yet until we are back to a new normal. As you approach voting age be sure to make your voices heard. If you are not happy with how things are being run in this country then don't be shy about this. My advice is ask for help (if you need it). Check up on your friends. Rest if you want – you don't have to be productive all the time. Let's keep going.

Wishing you all the best,

Dr Lia 😊

Dr Lia Jones is a newly qualified junior doctor who graduated in summer 2020 in the middle of the pandemic

Emily Fosbraey

Dear World,

Things are difficult here in lockdown. For starters, everything has changed: I've not been able to see my friends, I've had to be homeschooled, and on top of all this, I've had OCD to deal with! It started in March when this whole Covid-19 thing began. I was touching and doing things obsessively that I just couldn't stop. It got worse and worse.

Then in late May I had my first CAMHS appointment, and the ladies I talked to were very nice and open to everything I had to say.

I continued having the sessions and began to feel quite comfortable talking about what I was dealing with. I was getting much better!

Now I don't have sessions anymore, but I think that when I did have them, my mental health improved a lot. I was helped to handle my situations one at a time and eventually got rid of them all.

My lockdown hasn't all been bad though!

I have done many fun activities and kept in touch with my friends.

I just want to say that you can get through anything, though it may take time.

Emily Fosbraey ☺
Age 10

Vicky Mills

Dear Young People,

I'd like to talk about uncertainty. Not knowing what is going to happen can give us anxiety, you know that feeling? Like your heartbeat goes quicker, you get hot, maybe even breathless and panicky. There has been so much uncertainty this year with Covid, however it has affected your life, and I am sure it has.

I write to you in the hope that you can use this experience and look back on it as a time that you coped with uncertainty. Whether you feel you coped well or not, you still coped to an extent. ('Coping' includes getting frustrated, angry or low. Even crying is a form of coping.) We often tell ourselves that we aren't coping but actually, even getting dressed is a sign of coping.

Covid is becoming part of your story as it is an event in your life which you will later look back on and talk about. Remember it as a time of managing that uncertainty - as let's face it, we've had no other option. Somehow we get on with it. That's coping. We all have a tremendous amount of emotional strength, which doesn't mean we don't feel weak or vulnerable, it just means we get through it. The clouds of emotions do pass with time. It might be helpful to even imagine you are sitting on top of the raincloud instead of being rained on.

Coping with uncertainty also includes asking for help. We aren't meant to cope alone - us humans are social creatures, we are stronger together. We will get through this together because as a species we have the emotional resources to do so.

Best wishes

Vicky

Vicky Mills works as a CBT therapist in private practice within Hampshire

Adam Fare

Dear Reader,

Life can throw us a mixture of emotions. We can go from a stage of unflappable high to demoralising low in an instant. The usual trials and tribulations of everyday living is something we all face, and the emotional turbulence is completely normal, especially as we develop and find who we are as humans and where we fit in this ever-changing world.

Then comes Covid.

Something out of the blue, out of the ordinary, and something which puts us very quickly into unchartered territory.

I have had an eating disorder now for twelve years of my life, since I was eleven years old.

Eating disorders can affect anyone, of any age, and any gender. They do not discriminate. Being a man with an eating disorder has been difficult. I have been hit with stigma, misunderstanding and, at times, blind denial that it is even possible (which at times even came from my own mind).

Now we come to the atomic bomb that has been Covid-19. The pandemic has created a plethora of changes, many of which have the potential to seriously affect those with eating disorders.

We start with the panic buying that came before the first lockdown. This created food insecurity and constant anxiety, worrying if I could get the food which was on my meal plan, that plan that is currently keeping me on the right path. It may seem strange, but not having those foods can seriously affect me. I have been lucky so far that I've had what I need, but that did not stop the sleepless nights worrying about it.

Then there was lockdown. Now eating disorders are illnesses that thrive in isolation, when it is just me, myself and I. I also live alone which makes for some interesting thoughts flying around in that racetrack of my brain sometimes. The routine change to working from home gave more opportunity to engage in unhealthy behaviours. I had no one else to be accountable to, and no one could see me either. I had to choose, every day, to fight that urge. To choose recovery at every turn and to never waver from the path that I am on. Even one little slip up could start a spiral.

Eating disorders, like any mental health illness, are not something anyone chooses to have, nor do they want to have one. However, we can choose to fight, we can choose to try, we can choose recovery over our illnesses.

My life now is filled with love, passion and drive. That drive being to make a real change to the lives of those who are struggling. If we all come together, we can make that change.

My final message: life may seem impossibly hard at times, but you deserve to be here. You deserve to take up the space you do. You deserve to be happy.

Adam

Adam Fare is a data analyst and campaigner for a fairer, happier and healthier society

Lily Wisdom

To my dear brother,

Even before the lockdown, you relied on routine and liked to know what you would be doing before each day and if that changed, it was very difficult for you. Sometimes you would wake up and feel very low and you wouldn't know why and then at night time you found it impossible to sleep because you would worry about different things. You described it as having a black cloud follow you around at times which made you feel like you hated yourself and you were always saying sorry for things you didn't need to. I didn't really understand why you felt this way as I had nothing to compare it to.

Then the Coronavirus arrived and turned all of our worlds upside down. It started slowly and then scary things were being said on the news. We were told that if we didn't stay at home and stay away from everyone including our family and friends, that we could catch the virus. And die. And this was so scary because you and Mum are in the high-risk group. Suddenly, very suddenly, everything changed. Dad stopped going to work, we stopped going to school and we had to stay in the house. I found school finishing a big shock but for you it must have been far worse. You were due to sit your GCSE exams and this had made you worry a lot about getting ready for them but you had been working so hard. You would have done your exams and then you would have had your leavers' assembly and your prom with all of your friends and then the freedom to meet your friends after all your hard work. This needed a lot of planning so that you could cope with every day but then BANG! it all changed. This sent you into a spin.

At home, you suffered, you were lost while we waited to hear what was going to happen. You couldn't watch the news because it made you panic and your anxiety became even worse. And I started to realise a little bit of how you must have been feeling for years. Because I felt panicky, angry, frustrated, nervous and sad. We knew that if Mum got the virus, she could get really ill and even die and the thought of losing family was the worst thing in the world. I couldn't sleep and have needed lots of hugs and reassurance. When Dad goes to the shops, we panic until he comes home and then watch him wash everything so that we are safe.

We've been in lockdown for about nine weeks now and I'm so proud of you. You have settled into our 'new normal' as best you can by finding things to keep you busy. We have found many projects to do outside in the garden and inside. Mum and Dad have been so grateful for our help, we've made a difference and that feels good. We have baked, played sports, cooked for Mum and Dad, walked, demolished and built, reorganised, and cared for the guinea pigs, making improvements to their runs.

I have noticed that we are checking on each other more and are talking about our feelings. It has been good to have Dad home more than he is normally because he works in London. I have enjoyed our time together, baking with Mum, Dad helping me with my basketball and just spending time with you. We have found ways to keep in touch with our friends - you on your PS4 and me on WhatsApp. We've been phoning our Nanna too as she is by herself and sending her and other people homemade cards.

I am so pleased that you have something to look forward to... because we are getting a puppy to help you and it's not long now until he comes to live with us. Thank you for being the best brother I could ever have wished for (most of the time!!!)

Lily Wisdom
Age 13

Hope Virgo

Dear Young People,

When we look back on history, there will be things that have changed massively due to a virus! A pandemic! It won't be like you may have seen in movies, but instead life tries to keep going on around it. There were weeks and months where there was so much uncertainty. Being a freelancer I had to accept that I lost work (and so did others), everyone was forced to slow down, and I felt things I haven't felt in a long time.

I was in recovery from anorexia at the time when the pandemic hit and, despite being eleven years out of hospital, I was still facing challenges and cracks along the way. The stockpiling of food was hard; this struggle to access foods that felt easy and safe. My main issue was around exercise! I had always used exercise in a healthy way in my recovery, but losing my routine with the gym felt tough. And to make it worse everyone started sharing their workouts online and I felt stuck in this competitive cycle. Never feeling good enough. Feeling disgusted in my body and myself. It took every amount of strength in me to keep going and to keep talking. To keep sharing my day-to-day feelings and emotions with those around me. It got easier as lockdown progressed; as I got stuck into a new way of life.

As lockdown began to ease and things gradually began to return to a new sense of normality, it still felt hard at times. But I knew I had to make sure that my recovery wouldn't be de-railed by a pandemic and comments from those around me. For once I had to make this about me, I had to put up healthy boundaries to protect myself.

It was hard, and I am not going to pretend it wasn't! It became a rollercoaster and at times it felt impossible to plan ahead. There were so many times when things felt like they would never be okay again. But each time these moments happened I had to remember all those moments of pure joy, from when they played the UK Blessing, to a 5.30am trip to the sea or when I ordered Deliveroo and the wrong meal came.

There was more laughing than crying and I came through it stronger!

Hope

Hope Virgo is the author of *Stand Tall Little Girl* and a mental health campaigner

Brianna Mvula

To Future Self,

I have adjusted to what has now been called 'the new normal'. I can chat to my friends either way who now all have mobile phones. I downloaded this new game called House Party and it's where you can call your friends on it while playing a game with them and it's really fun.

I now know how to go onto Microsoft Teams and Zoom by myself. I am also learning how to walk to school by myself so that when I go back to school, I can go to school and back on my own.

Yours sincerely,

Brianna Mvula

Emily Grace

Dear Future Self,

Do you remember the global pandemic that swept across the world in 2020? Weeks before the pandemic reached the UK you had started a new role at a local hospital; little did you know the chaos that was about to ensue.

As the country went into lockdown, the message from the government was clear: stay home, save lives, protect the NHS. Schools, restaurants, cinemas, sports centres, and most shops closed their doors for an unknown time frame and the government encouraged people to work from home.

However, working on medical wards in an acute hospital you were classed as a "key worker" and so to some degree life continued as normal for you. Rainbows became a universally recognised symbol to thank key workers, reminding everyone that storms don't last forever. People set up support funds, companies sent donations to be handed out to workers. Each Thursday evening at 8pm people stood on their doorsteps and clapped the key workers.

In five short months more than 41,000 people in the UK lost their lives to Covid-19. Amidst the pain and suffering, if you looked closely it also brought many benefits; pollution rates were down, rivers ran clear and thick smog that hung over many cities began to clear. Many lessons were learnt.

It was hard for many families spending time apart from loved ones, but families in the same household were spending quality time together. People furloughed from work undertook numerous projects, ranging from household repairs and distance learning courses to personal health and fitness challenges.

Covid-19 stressed a lot of people, but it reminded everyone how resilient, adaptable, and creative we are. Postal workers dressed as superhero characters, and one household set up giant teddy bears doing a different activity each day. One local family dressed as dinosaurs, dancing around the streets to amuse children and boost morale. I created a scavenger hunt for the local children to occupy them on their daily walks. Random acts of kindness were everywhere, with people donating items to those less fortunate than themselves.

As the lockdown restrictions eased, I was able to genuinely appreciate so many things I had previously taken for granted. The ability to sit down and enjoy a meal with family or the luxury of being able to take my gran for a coffee. Never again would I let my life get so busy that I forgot about what really mattered to me, because now I had seen that in the blink of an eye those opportunities really could be gone forever.

Best wishes,

Emily

Emily Grace is a mental health ambassador and charity trustee

Poppy Lacey

Dear Future Self,

Yes this situation SUCKED, yes we all wished 2020 never happened but we all did it together! During lockdown, I started to explore new ways to keep myself and my immediate family entertained. We played board games, took part in virtual quizzes and I got to do more of what I loved: writing. I entered national competitions and one time, I actually got published!

Poppy Lacey
Age 13

Chloe Bartholomew

Dear Dad,

Thank you for staying positive throughout 2020. The forest fires, World War Three threats, panic buying and of course, Covid. I wanted to say how proud of you I was for still going out because of your job. You're one of the most amazing people I know! I didn't see you too much before Covid was here, but once it arrived I saw you even less because you had to work overtime. Home school wasn't bad but it was really stressful for Mum which is imaginable. When we went out on Thursdays to clap, I wasn't just clapping for the NHS, bus drivers, people working in shops or at tills, I was clapping for you.

Love Chloe 🖤 Bartholomew
Age 12

Lucas Ongley

It's making me feel lonely
Just let me out this house and be free
When I do go outside for my exercise it's like a ghost town
You could search for miles and wouldn't find anyone around

Lucas Ongley
Age 15

Ansh Jhawar

Dear Dadu and Dadi,

How are you both doing? Hope you are both safe and not going out into tons of crowds in India. How did you spend your Diwali in lockdown? Did you step out to burst crackers? Did you buy a lot of sweets from the mithai shop?

Last year Diwali was very different for us and quite unusual due to COVID-19. Usually, we invite friends to our house to eat food and share our sweets or we go to their houses and have Diwali parties. We also used to have big gatherings where I would participate on the stage but last year we didn't do anything like that. A few days before Diwali, Mummy and Daddy always took me to Southampton Hindu temple or London Swaminarayan temple but last year again due to lockdown we didn't go anywhere and we performed the entire puja at home.

We decorated the house. It was gleaming beautifully bright with lights and more fairy lights everywhere. It looked really pretty. I even made rangoli using powder colours outside our front door with different patterns. On the Diwali morning, Mummy always gives me an oil massage and bath which smells really nice and reminds us all of India. We also light one sparkler outside in the garden of our building as it denotes good luck. The sparklers that I bought from Aldi were called 'Boom Boom Blaster'.

During lockdown, on the Diwali day, we did a lot of Zoom calls to all my friends and family across the globe to give them our Diwali wishes. My mummy also participated in an online Diwali competition organised in Southampton and won third prize and we were all so happy. I also clicked lots of photos. In the evening we went downstairs in the garden and lit a couple of sparkles and came back home. We all had yummy food that Mummy made like Chickpea Curry (Chole), Indian Cottage Cheese (Butter Paneer Masala), Lentils (Tadka Daal) and loads of snacks like Ladoo, etc. It was the best meal ever!! Mummy also let me light all the diyas in the house and it was so much fun to do it. I also wrote a small fun poem:

Diwali is the Festival of Light,
All the Diyas are shining bright.
Light sparkles,
sound crackles.
I make Rangolis and eat Mithai,
Nothing rhymes, so I use the word 'Samurai'.

Hope you like my poem Dadu and Dadi. I don't want to celebrate Diwali again in lockdown. I really wish and pray that I could join you for Diwali this year or you could perhaps come here. Please take care of yourself and do not go to crowded places. Love you lots...

Yours always,

Ansh Jhawar
Age 7

Jordan Fewings

Dear Future Me,

How is the world? Is it still a mess? Is Corona still causing chaos throughout the world? Please tell me it gets better. Please tell me I get to see my family again, I miss them.

2020 had too many negative things happening: forest fires in Australia, America and Iran almost starting a war, an explosion in Lebanon that caused 300,000 people to become homeless and that is scratching the surface of the massive list. Please tell me it gets better?

This year has been hard for everyone, no one was safe either from Corona or from mental health issues. Too many people have lost their lives whether it was taken from them or cut short due to being in lockdown. I just want it to go back to how it was near the end of last year, when everyone's big worry was about what they wanted for dinner, if they could be bothered to cook, or order a pizza. It seems like a distant memory now. Please tell me it gets better.

Mental health difficulties have spiked this year, for me included. I was getting better too before this all happened. Being locked indoors or not being able to see friends or family can play a massive part in your mental state not knowing when you will see them again. When you read this please tell me we have found a cure for Corona, or better yet mental health issues. Please tell me it gets better.

Jordan Fewings
Age 23

Chris Wild

Dear Reader,

I had a call through on my phone from reception asking me to make my way to the main office. The Roundhouse was buzzing with young people taking part in all sorts of projects. I was working on the Spoken Word programme with ten amazing young people.

There was lots of commotion coming from the main meeting room. I was now very anxious. Surely, I was not getting fired? I had only just started.

I made my way in and sat down at the table.

The CEO began to speak.

'I am sorry to announce that from 6pm tonight The Roundhouse will be stopping all its programmes, and everyone will be working from home.'

I collected my laptop and left.

Two weeks later I was made redundant. Reason? Covid-19.

Lockdown was a bit of a shock for me. It took me a few weeks to accept it. I am a physical person and even if I am resting, I am working. But it was not about me, I was more concerned about all the young people who came to The Roundhouse to escape. Those from disadvantaged backgrounds looking to create a future for themselves. And just like that they were tossed back out into the streets with a bag full of uncertainty.

For the first month I made it about me. I was not thinking straight. I was not in the right frame of mind. So I drank copious amounts of wine. The news made me feel sick and the noise from the street was deafening. Children bored, screaming, playing. Music blaring from windows like they had misunderstood the lockdown. It was not a national holiday. It was a lockdown. People were dying, people were being made redundant.

Depression kicked in rather quickly, but I soon woke up to the reality of this life, the new way of living. By the second month I had managed to crawl back out of my cave, and I started to focus on real issues.

I volunteered to help local organisations and charities deliver food packages to young people living in semi-independent care, those who had no support, no family, no money, and no professional help.

How do I want to remember my lockdown?

By forgetting about my selfish behaviour and remembering my objective in life, which is to help young people in the care sector, as I was once one of them.

Chris

Chris Wild grew up in the care system and later worked in a care home himself He is now an artist, actor and author of *Damaged*, and continues to work on many campaigns for young people in the care sector

Daria Rose Gibson

Dear Mrs Franson,

I am writing to tell you that I miss you so much and you mean so much to me. This quarantine has made these months the hardest of my life. I started off with moving to London from America. I moved with my family: two sisters, parents, and dog. One reason we moved was to see and be closer to our extended family. Unfortunately this was and still is not possible which makes me feel disappointed, sad, and alone.

When we finally found a school, after only a few months it had been changed to online schooling which affected my education in many ways. The hardest thing was not being able to have a teacher by my side to help me and guide me to learning new things. This was especially difficult for the practical lessons. I also miss playing sports. Amazingly the teachers have been so kind and considerate. Before moving to online school, I would not see many people helping others as much or even more than themselves. This is why I am so grateful for teachers like you!

Although the lockdown has been extremely difficult and upsetting, there have been some positives. Zoom has been great for international ballet classes, continuing playing my instruments, and starting our new Sunday family quiz. During the lockdown I improved on my typing skills. I have also started doing more arts, crafts and reading.

Soon Christmas is coming. Despite the lockdown, I had been happier than ever as Christmas is one of my favourite holidays. I was excited for many reasons: delicious food, getting to see family after a long time, board games, being able to see people I know other than my close family, not having to wear a mask in another place other than my home, and so much more. All of a sudden we heard that the Prime Minister was going to give an announcement. When the time came, we turned on the TV and listened. Christmas would be cancelled! Disappointed as our bags were packed ready to go, we slowly descended to the kitchen to have dinner. It was silent for a bit. After a while as we were all upset, someone finally spoke. Trying not to ruin everyone's mood too much, we tried to do as much as we could to make each other happy. Finally, Christmas day arrived. It was an amazing day and I got everything I wanted. From then on it has been a good day ever since.

As you can see, things do not need to be planned to be happy.

I hope you are doing well,

Daria Rose Gibson
Age 11

Liza Nahajski

Dear Reader,

I love Christmas! I love the excitement, the tinsel, the carols, the parties, midnight mass, presents, turkey... pretty much all of it! Maybe that is why I got an invitation to help organise Christmas in our parish.

First, three of us (including our priest) met on Zoom to discuss how we were going to help get the Christmas message of hope out to people. We were particularly concerned for families with young children and those who were feeling the grim presence of the pandemic. Could we lift people's spirits in the festive season?

So many things were strange. Seats at mass were booked online with places snapped up as if it was Glastonbury ticket release day. We built a pallet stable and a star trail to allow for some fun for the children outdoors, and Facebook was buzzing with the nativity pictures (and animations) from creative families around the parish.

All this absorbed my waking hours and by Christmas week I realised I hadn't really done much Christmas shopping. Panic buying was all that remained two days before Christmas. I remember wandering around Winchester searching for a vacuum flask for my daughter's boyfriend. It felt as if the world was folding up around me. The emptying discount shelves of Debenhams gave a sad January sales feel to the city. I bought packs of socks and discount pillows. The glitter and baubles seemed tawdry as masked shoppers moved anxiously around. The anticipation of walks with friends and a small gathering with relatives had been dashed by Boris. The chill in the air penetrated deep.

On Christmas Eve my family would normally gather with our Polish relatives to celebrate Wigelia. We all love the food and our families normally share out preparation of the twelve-course meal between us. At my mother-in-law's house we crowd onto sofas and chairs for a reading of the nativity of Jesus and a prayer followed by a spontaneous round of hugs, kisses and greetings as we share the oplatki, breaking a small corner off each other's Christmas wafer embossed with the Nativity scene. We all say "Happy Christmas!" or

"I hope you have a great year!" and so on as we weave amongst each other and try to remember who we have missed. The meal takes forever and the conversation rolls with ample quantities of vodka poured into tiny vodka glasses.

In 2020 Zoom was our gathering space and the boxes were crowded with family groups and couples as we listened to the reading and prayer, and greeted each other with mimed hugs and kisses before departing to our own versions of the Wigilia feast. We had booked in for 10pm mass and walked through the deserted streets of Winchester in the chill air. With masks on, we signed in at church (track and trace), and were shown to the socially distanced seats designated for us. Mass was simple, cold (with the open doors) and deeply moving. There was no communal singing, no crowded aisles, and just one reader to avoid contamination. It was beautiful. I felt as if I was a privileged shepherd in a dingy stable, I felt as if God had quietly entered into his own creation and I happened to be there to see it. As Father Mark preached and we heard again that Emmanuel means 'God is with us'
it was clear the pandemic cannot cancel Christmas after all.

Liza

Liza Nahajski is a parishioner at her local Catholic church

Isabella Barton

Dear 29-year-old Me,

I don't really know what I will be doing at 29 years of age. I can't imagine being that old! Will I be a Lego designer, a rat breeder or a small animal vet? I hope that I am happy (and have lots of pet rats!). I hope that I am healthy.

As a nine year old, I can describe this past year as traumatic, fast, different, peculiar. We have been living through a pandemic. We have had national lockdowns, been told to stay at home, been told to go to school as it is safe, done remote learning, been into school as a child of key worker parents and I have washed my hands until they are red raw! We have painted rainbows, clapped for carers and not been to parties or sleepovers for ages.

The most famous person of this past year has been Professor Chris Whitty. He has helped everyone understand the medical advice to keep safe during this pandemic. We had 'bubbles' of people we lived with and supported. Mummy, Daddy and I are in a bubble with Granny and Grandad who live nearby. They help us by looking after me when Mummy and Daddy work and also Granny needs help as she is disabled.

I haven't been worried during the pandemic about Covid specifically. I didn't think we would catch it because we were staying at home so much. I thought Mummy and Daddy would be safe at work as they don't take risks at home.

Christmas was a very different one. We couldn't see any friends or family other than on Zoom calls which we arranged. We had our decorations up from the end of November and still have our lights up today (19th January!) because it keeps our spirits high.

Over Christmas Mummy and Daddy started to feel unwell. Although they were poorly they didn't have any Covid symptoms so weren't able to get a test, however someone from Mummy's work rang to say they were Covid positive and then things happened pretty quickly. Mummy and Daddy got tested and they were positive and then Granny and Grandad became unwell. I suddenly lost my sense of smell. I had a strange rash on my chin and our family doctor asked me to take a home test.

The home test was very tricky – it tickled my throat and nose so much. We had been indoors for so many days but were allowed out to walk to the post box with the test. It was like being free and a breath of fresh air!

My test came back positive too. I was a bit surprised but I wasn't worried because we were all feeling better. I was worried about Granny and Grandad because they are older. Grandad went to hospital but he didn't stay for long and came back home to recover. He and Granny are both a bit better. I made them small jellies and mince pies to tempt them to eat!

Although I am only nine years old, I have coped with the past year and all it has thrown at us. I am stronger than I think I am. I hope the 29-year-old me realises that I can do things even when there's a world crisis. I just need to find the small things in life – they are there all the time but you need to be open minded to look for them. These small things will give you hope and joy.

Love from,

Isabella Barton xxx
Age 9

Matthew Stanton

Dear Future Matthew,

Since March 2020, I have been in lockdown with my mum, my dad and my older brother.

The main thing that I have been doing is schoolwork, but it was not easy. At first, my school had no idea what to do, seeing as it was a first that a life-threatening virus was on the loose. We had very little work to do and had no help from teachers or classmates. Because of this, my parents sent me to isolation school (because my dad is a key worker) and got me two tutors to stay on track with my education. After the first wave of lockdown my family got a letter. I could go back to school. This was it! I could finally get back to my education after six months of being in a global prison. Frustratingly, two weeks into school, I was put in a room and told that one of my classmates had Coronavirus. My heart dropped. I was shocked knowing that I had to be stuck inside for two weeks again. Knowing that I wasn't allowed to see my friends and family. Knowing that I was back in prison.

Unfortunately, this was not my last self-isolation. I had another two within the autumn term because of people around me catching the virus: my classmate, my brother and my best friend. At the time I was wondering if there was ever going to be a time where I wasn't stuck inside.

Having been trapped, I had to make the most of it. I have been learning different genres on my guitar and spending more time with my brother. Being able to connect with my brother amazed us both. This is because, normally, I never see him; he is always out, enjoying time with his friends. Having quality time with my brother has made us happier.

Sadly, there have been many lows in this time. While locked up, there is one major thing I am missing... football. I feel a big decrease in my fitness and stamina just because I can't play the sport I love. As well as this, I have not been able to test out my new football boots that I got for Christmas.

Speaking of Christmas, the day was a bit different this year. On the 23rd December we got the news from our Prime Minister that we couldn't spend Christmas with our extended family. We were all fed up.

Having said this, we weren't going to give up. We got as many decorations as humanly possible and splashed out on presents. So, future me, is my next Christmas normal?

Matthew Stanton
Age 13

Zara Bhhakar

My birthday was the first day of lockdown and we couldn't do anything as everything was closed and I didn't even go to school as that was closed as well but my family really did make it the most amazing birthday.

Zara Bhhakar
Age 13

Charlotte Slinger

Dear Babies of 2020/2021,

What an extraordinary start you've had being born during a global pandemic. You are a 'once in a generation' generation, born in unprecedented times, despite all the external struggles and restrictions. You remind us that life persists and humanity evolves, regardless of suffering, sickness and challenge. You bring with you vitality, hope and newness. Welcome to this complicated, beautiful world!

I wonder what you'll take with you from this unexpected year as you grow up? I hope you don't remember the fear, isolation and separation of these strange times and never have to live through them again. I hope your bond with your parent/s, carers and family is strong and special because of the intense time you've spent locked down together. I hope that you and your family could access help if you needed it. I hope you have time to develop deep relationships with your wider family and community when it's possible to spend time together again. Mostly I hope that you can still become who you are meant to be.

How will the pandemic affect your next few years? I wonder if you'll ever share sticky, tattered toys with multiple children at a playgroup, or joyously blow out candles on a birthday cake, or spontaneously reach for the hand of a new friend in the park? Hopefully we don't over-sanitise your childhood or deny you the fun of getting messy.

Even though we worry that you have had too much digital interaction too soon, perhaps you'll view technology as a great enabler and develop future technological breakthroughs? Even though we worry that you haven't had enough social interaction, perhaps you'll grow to be more socially sensitive, be able to navigate public space with natural respect and awareness and find innovative ways of building friendships and communities, perhaps be able to read over-the-mask expressions with instant ease? Even though we worry you have missed out on a 'normal' start, perhaps you'll grow to be more resilient, self-reliant and strong than we could imagine.

Thank you for helping us focus on life and new beginnings, for helping us stay in the moment and be grateful for simple things like a smile, a giggle and a cuddle.

Oh, and in years to come, when you're older, ask your family about this time. And perhaps thank them. However hard it was, they did their best and muddled through. Everyone's experience is individual and this has been an extremely hard time to be a new parent, but despite the challenge and the exhaustion of isolation, you're worth it.

With love,

Charlotte

Charlotte Slinger became a new mother in October 2019 and went into lockdown with a five month old

Arsh Agrawal

Dear Covid Warriors,

Hurray for the NHS. Thanks for saving our lives during the Pandemic. You have done a lot for us. Well done NHS. You have worked continuously without break or holidays. We know it's very difficult to work with full PPE kits and working hard for patients whilst your own life is in danger.

Thank you, Mr Prime Minister, for taking difficult and correct decisions for our country. Even though you had Covid-19 and fought for your life, you took great care of the country and its citizens.

Thanks to all school teachers and headteachers for supporting us in this pandemic. You gave activity packs so we could keep ourselves busy at home and boost our knowledge and skill throughout the lockdown. You always wore masks to keep everyone safe. You made small bubbles and worked hard for each bubble.

Thanks to all council workers who collect bins. In such a worrying situation, you always came and collected the waste, which helped us to maintain our hygiene and health. I saw from my house window, you always started early at 6:30am, which is really appreciated. You have done really hard and great work for the nation.

Thanks to all essential shop keepers as you gave us essential items whenever we needed them. The shops were always open for needy people. You also helped us a lot by delivering items at our doorstep. We never struggled for the essential things at our places because you guys were always there for us.

Thanks to the police, for keeping us safe. You worked hard. You were alert at night so we could sleep peacefully.

Thank you scientists, for developing the vaccine so quickly. You found it quickly without stopping. Well done.

Thank you so much all of you for your hard work and dedication to our nation. Our country will never forget your sacrifice in this tough time. You all made a team and worked hard to help the country in

fighting against this stressful condition.

With regards,

Arsh Agrawal
Age 8

Marnie McKensie

Dear Future Marnie,

I'm writing to you in hope of reminding you what your COVID-19 experience was like. Is COVID-19 over? I'm hoping that by the time you receive this, it will be. Feel free to get emotional.

The first lockdown had me feeling really low. I felt alone and thought no one would understand.

The only thing I could look forward to was seeing a few of my close friends. Most days, my friends Rosa and Sadie would come round to the park near my house and we would talk. Often about nothing. I remember one particular day when we had all held off crying and our emotions had just built up. We just cried. We sat behind a bush and just hugged and cried. We stayed like that for hours. Being able to let out all my emotions and stresses with them felt so good. I knew I could trust them not to tell anyone.

I realised that it wasn't healthy to let it all build up inside me, so I started having small chats about how I was feeling with my mum. That really helped me. I don't think I would have been able to keep it together without that. I am so thankful to them and love them all. Every evening, at around eight o'clock my mum, my sister and I would go to the local park to play table tennis. It was our small treat at the end of the day; we all enjoyed it.

After the summer holiday, I started secondary school. It was all quite normal, except for having to socially distance. Those few months went really fast and soon it was the Christmas holidays.

Then we got the news of a third lockdown. It was devastating. Any dreams of having a regular year were demolished. Online school started. It wasn't too bad. It meant I got to have lie-ins and did not have to walk to school in the cold. As January went on, I started to feel mentally and physically sick. Still now I have to sit at a computer all day and often won't go out for days. It's becoming harder as we are set more and more work. When I am in online classes, it is so frustrating because many students have technical difficulties, which makes it hard to learn. There are so many emotions swirling around in my head: stress, anxiety and fatigue. It's hard. Impossible. I'm not sure how much longer I can last in this kind of situation.

Yours sincerely,

Marnie McKensie
Age 12

Georgina Atkinson

Dear Me,

Remember lockdown? Remember that crazy, whirlwind of a time? No? Well that means you're remembering it right. No, you didn't learn something new. No, you didn't change the world. No you didn't make a difference.

But that's fine, you may not have learnt a new language, started baking amazing meals, joined in protests or saved the planet but you did progress in one language, helped in the kitchen, educated yourself on the world and tried your best to recycle.

You had your ups and downs, in school, life, friendships, family. But it all shaped you into the person you needed to be to survive lockdown. And remember you did survive.

Don't lie when they ask you about your experiences, embrace your humanity. Remember your successes and low points.

Remember your lockdown.

Remember,

Me

Georgina Atkinson
Age 14

Resources for Young People

Websites

Hampshire CAMHS website: www.hampshirecamhs.nhs.uk

Young Minds: youngminds.org.uk

The Mix: www.themix.org.uk

CalmZone: www.thecalmzone.net

Papyrus: www.papyrus-uk.org

Phone/Text

Call Childline: 0800 1111
(Free to call, 24 hours a day, 7 days a week)

Call Hopeline: 0800 068 4141
(Free to call, 9am-midnight, 7 days a week)

Text Hopeline: 07860 039 967
(Free to text, 9am-midnight, 7 days a week)

Young Minds Text Messenger Service: text YM to 85258
(Free to text, 24 hours a day, 7 days a week)

Text Chat Health: 07507 332 160
(Response time: Within 24 hours, 8.30am to 4.30pm Monday to
Friday-except bank holidays)

Apps to download

What's Up
The Fabulous Daily Self-Care App
Teen Smart Goals App
Stay Alive
Stop Think Breathe
Fear Tools
Mood Tools

Resources for Parents/Carers

Websites

Hampshire CAMHS website: www.hampshirecamhs.nhs.uk

Anna Freud Centre: www.annafreud.org

Family Lives: www.familylives.org.uk

Young Minds Parents Help: youngminds.org.uk/find-help/for-parents

Phone/Text

Samaritans: 116 123
(Free to call, 24 hours a day, 7 days a week)

Mental Health Triage Service: call 111 (Free to call 24 hours a day, 7 days a week)
or visit www.111.nhs.uk and speak to the NHS Mental Health Triage Service.

Family Lives Parent Support: 0808 800 2222
(Free to call, Monday- Friday 9am-9pm; Weekends 10am-3pm)

Young Minds Parent Helpline: 0808 802 5544 (Free to call, Monday-Friday 9.30am-4pm)

Text Shout: 85258
(Free to text, 24 hours a day, 7 days a week)

Resources for Professionals

Websites

Hampshire CAMHS website: www.hampshirecamhs.nhs.uk

Anna Freud Centre: www.annafreud.org

MindED website: www.minded.org.uk

Phone/Text

Samaritans: 116 123 (Free to call 24 hours a day, 7 days a week)

Education Support Partnership Helpline Number: 08000 562 561 or text: 07909 341229 (Free 24 hours a day, 7 days a week)

Mental Health Triage Service: call 111 (Free to call 24 hours a day, 7 days a week) or visit www.111.nhs.uk and speak to the NHS Mental Health Triage Service.

Acknowledgments

Hampshire CAMHS would like to thank the wonderful selection panel for volunteering their time on this project.

Abi Barnes

Abi is a local young person who has previously accessed Hampshire CAMHS services. She was a young person representative on the panel.

Susmita Bhattacharya

Susmita Bhattacharya is a writer and lecturer at the University of Winchester. She has published a novel, *The Normal State of Mind* (Parthian, 2015) and *Table Manners* (Dahlia Books, 2019) which won the Saboteur Best Short Story Collection Prize. She also facilitates ArtfulScribe's Mayflower Young Writers programme in Southampton.

Judith Heneghan

Dr Judith Heneghan is a writer, editor and Senior Lecturer in Creative Writing at the University of Winchester. She has written over 60 books for young people and her first novel for adults, *Snegurochka*, was published by Salt in 2019. She has four grown-up children.

Charlotte Slinger

Charlotte is passionate about using arts, creativity and culture for positive social impact, particularly with young people. She is a freelance arts consultant, based in Hampshire, advising cultural organisations on strategy, partnerships and fundraising.